JELLYFISH
IN THE WATER

CLARA COLEMAN

PowerKiDS press™

New York

Published in 2018 by The Rosen Publishing Group, Inc.
29 East 21st Street, New York, NY 10010

First Edition

Editor: Melissa Raé Shofner
Book Design: Tanya Dellaccio

Photo Credits: Cover Oxford Scientific/Getty Images; pp. 3–24 (background image) Kemal Mardin/Shutterstock.com; pp. 5, 13 (bottom) H. Tanaka/Shutterstock.com; p. 7 (top) Alessandro Di Filippo/Shutterstock.com; p. 7 (bottom) Damsea/Shutterstock.com; p. 8 Kristina Vackova/Shutterstock.com; p. 9 Alexander Semenov/Moment Open/Getty Images; p. 11 (top) James Forte/National Geographic Magazines/Getty Images; p. 11 (bottom) LagunaticPhoto/Shutterstock.com; p. 13 (top) EloyMR/Shutterstock.com; p. 15 David Wrobel/Visuals Unlimited/Getty Images; p. 16 archana bhartia/Shutterstock.com; p. 17 Richard Herrmann/Minden Pictures/Getty Images; p. 19 (top) Alexander Semenov/Moment/Getty Images; p. 19 (bottom) Olya Steckel/Shutterstock.com; p. 21 Chai Seamaker/Shutterstock.com; p. 22 Rada Photos/Shutterstock.com.

Cataloging-in-Publication Data

Names: Coleman, Clara.
Title: Jellyfish in the water / Clara Coleman.
Description: New York : PowerKids Press, 2018. | Series: Critters by the sea | Includes index.
Identifiers: LCCN ISBN 9781538325858 (pbk.) | ISBN 9781538325155 (library bound) | ISBN 9781538325865 (6 pack)
Subjects: LCSH: Jellyfishes–Juvenile literature.
Classification: LCC QL377.S4 C65 2018 | DDC 593.5'3–dc23

Manufactured in the United States of America

CPSIA Compliance Information: Batch #BW18PK: For Further Information contact Rosen Publishing, New York, New York at 1-800-237-9932

CONTENTS

NOT MADE OF JELLY!

Jellyfish have a strange name. They aren't fish, and they aren't made of jelly! However, they do live in the ocean, as many fish do. The shiny, soft bodies of some jellyfish do look a lot like jelly, but they're made mostly of water.

Jellyfish belong to one of the most common groups of animals in the sea, Cnidaria. "Cnidaria" means "nettle." Nettles are plants known for their sting. Jellyfish also sting. Their stings can be very painful, and some are even deadly.

SEA CREATURE FEATURE

There are more than 2,000 species, or kinds, of jellyfish!

Jellyfish can be beautiful creatures. Don't get too close, though, or you might get a painful sting!

STRANGE BODIES

A jellyfish's bell, or body, is filled with water. This water **supports** its body similar to how air fills a balloon. Without water to fill its bell, a jellyfish will die. Jellyfish move themselves forward through the ocean by pushing water through their bell.

Tentacles and long tubes called oral arms hang beneath most jellyfish bells. Jellyfish use their tentacles to catch food. They use their oral arms to bring food to their mouth on the bottom of their bell.

SEA CREATURE FEATURE

The only opening on a jellyfish's body is its mouth. The mouth is used for both eating and returning waste to the ocean.

Jellyfish breathe through their skin. Many jellies have skin so thin you can see right through it!

BIG, LITTLE, UPSIDE DOWN!

Thimble jellyfish are one of the smallest species of jellyfish in the world. They grow only to about 1 inch (2.5 cm) wide. These tiny jellies are known for their sting, which can leave swimmers with a red **rash**.

Upside-down jellyfish live in waters near the shore. They lie on the ocean floor upside down. Their moving tentacles look like seaweed. **Algae** live in their tentacles and make their own food using sunlight. Algae share the food they make with the upside-down jellyfish in which they live.

SEA CREATURE FEATURE

Jellyfish were around millions of years before the dinosaurs. Those swimming in Earth's oceans today look very similar to those that lived there long ago.

UPSIDE-DOWN JELLYFISH

The largest species of jellyfish in the world is the lion's mane jellyfish. These jellies can grow up to 8 feet (2.4 m) wide. Their tentacles may be more than 100 feet (30.5 m) long.

A SEA OF LIGHTS

Some species of jellyfish are bioluminescent. This means they can produce light in their bodies. Jellyfish produce light for a number of reasons. Some use light to draw other jellyfish to them when they're ready to have babies.

Since jellyfish are slow swimmers that often just drift along with the ocean, it can be hard for them to catch a meal. Some may use their light to **attract** their **prey**. Once a fish or another small sea creature comes close enough, a jellyfish can eat it.

SEA CREATURE FEATURE

Crystal jellyfish use bioluminescence. They live in the Pacific Ocean along the coast of North America from Alaska to Baja California in Mexico.

It may look like these crystal jellyfish are glowing all over, but they're not. These jellies are nearly colorless but often appear to glow in photographs. Only a ring of body parts around the edge of their bell actually glows with bioluminescence.

JELLYFISH AROUND THE WORLD

Jellyfish are found around the world. Some species, such as lion's mane jellies, live in cold Arctic waters. Others, such as upside-down jellies, live in warm **tropical** waters. Some jellyfish live along coasts, while others live very deep in the ocean.

Jellyfish often drift where the ocean takes them. When the ocean pulls a huge group together, it's called a bloom. Blooms can be beautiful, but don't get too close if you see one. They're a danger to swimmers. A bloom may contain 100,000 jellyfish!

SEA CREATURE FEATURE

Sometimes jellyfish form blooms themselves. On the darkest night of the month, thousands of box jellyfish come together near the shore in Hawaii to **mate**.

Fried egg jellyfish, such as the one shown here, live in the Mediterranean Sea and the Atlantic Ocean. They're also called Mediterranean jellyfish.

JELLYFISH BLOOM

BABY JELLIES

After mating, a female jellyfish lays thousands of eggs. She carries the eggs for a few days until the larvae inside are ready to **hatch**.

Only a few of the larvae will make it to the ocean floor. There, they fix themselves to rocks or seaweed and turn into **polyps**. As polyps, they grow long stems that end in a ring of tentacles around one mouth. Soon, the top part of the polyp begins to split off. Tiny jellyfish break free and float away.

SEA CREATURE FEATURE

Adult jellyfish are called medusas. Larvae and medusas don't look anything alike.

When a young jellyfish breaks off from a polyp, it's called an ephyra.

DANGEROUS DARTS

To catch their food, jellyfish use special stinging cells called nematocysts. Each nematocyst has a tiny, poisonous dart inside. When a fish brushes against a nematocyst, the tiny dart shoots out. The poison makes the fish unable to swim. Sometimes, it even kills the fish.

A jellyfish may sting with hundreds of its nematocysts. For people, most jellyfish stings are simply painful. However, some jellyfish stings may be deadly. A sting from certain kinds of box jellyfish can kill a person in under 15 minutes.

SEA CREATURE FEATURE

Jellyfish may have nematocysts on their oral arms, tentacles, or mouth.

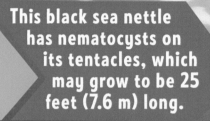

This black sea nettle has nematocysts on its tentacles, which may grow to be 25 feet (7.6 m) long.

TIME TO EAT

Jellyfish like to eat shrimp, fish, and other small sea animals. Most jellyfish wait for their prey to come to them. Species that feed on larger prey tend to have long tentacles covered with many nematocysts. They sting their prey so it can't swim, then slowly bring it to their mouth through their oral arms.

Some jellyfish eat **plankton**. These jellyfish often have sticky skin and tentacles with tiny hairs. Plankton are pushed past a jellyfish's mouth by the tentacle hairs and become trapped on its sticky skin.

SEA CREATURE FEATURE

Many species of jellyfish will often eat other species of jellyfish!

Jellyfish will eat pretty much anything that crosses their path in the ocean. Jellyfish blooms sometimes cause problems because they don't leave any food for fish to eat!

HARMFUL, BUT HELPFUL

A jellyfish's poisonous nematocysts actually help certain other sea creatures. Sea slugs, for example, have a special coating that keeps jellyfish stings from hurting them. This coating lets them keep jellyfish nematocysts on their back and use them to sting other predators.

Jellyfish have a special coating to keep from being stung by their own nematocysts. Tiny fish often swim beneath jellyfish and cover themselves in this coating, which **protects** them from the jellyfish's sting. The fish can then stay under the jellyfish for protection from other predators.

SEA CREATURE FEATURE

Some types of crabs will carry an upside-down jellyfish on their back. The jellyfish hides the crab and protects it by stinging predators that get too close.

Sea turtles love to eat jellyfish. Sadly, they sometimes mistakenly eat trash, such as plastic bags, that looks like jellyfish. Some types of crabs and fish eat jellyfish, too.

PEOPLE AND JELLIES

Jellyfish are high in **protein**, which is something humans need to live. With so many jellyfish in the ocean, some people think jellyfish would be a good food supply for the world's hungry people. In many Asian countries, jellies are a prized food.

Jellyfish are beautiful and interesting animals, but they can be dangerous. To safely look at jellyfish up close, you can visit an aquarium. There, you can view these underwater wonders without worrying about being stung.

GLOSSARY

algae: Living plantlike things that are mostly found in water.

attract: To draw nearer.

hatch: To break open or come out of.

mate: To come together to make babies.

plankton: A tiny plant or animal that floats in the ocean.

polyp: A type of animal with a fixed base, a tubelike body, and a free end with a mouth and tentacles.

prey: An animal hunted by other animals for food.

protect: To keep safe.

protein: A long chain of structural matter made by the body that helps a cell perform major functions.

rash: A group of red spots on the skin.

support: To hold up and help.

tentacle: A long, thin body part that sticks out from an animal's head or mouth.

tropical: Having to do with an area of the world known for warm and wet weather.

INDEX

WEBSITES

Due to the changing nature of Internet links, PowerKids Press has developed an online list of websites related to the subject of this book. This site is updated regularly. Please use this link to access the list:
www.powerkidslinks.com/seac/jelly

TITLES IN
THIS SERIES

CLAMS IN THE SAND
CRABS ON THE BEACH
JELLYFISH IN THE WATER
SEA GULLS IN THE SKY
SEA LIONS ON THE SHORE
SEA STARS IN THE TIDE POOL

GRL: N

AMERICAN READING COMPANY
Marine Life
www.americanreading.com

ISBN: 9...
6-pack ISBN...

9 781538 325858